Bathrooms

30 instant bathroom transformations

Bathrooms

30 instant bathroom transformations

Stewart & Sally Walton

Sebastian Kelly

First published in 1999 by
Sebastian Kelly

© Anness Publishing Limited 1999

Produced by Anness Publishing Limited

ISBN 1 84081 266 4

Publisher: Joanna Lorenz
Senior editor: Lindsay Porter
Photographer: Graham Rae
Designer: Simon Wilder
Jacket designer: Clare Baggeley

Printed in Hong Kong/China

1 3 5 7 9 10 8 6 4 2

CONTENTS

INTRODUCTION

MOST PEOPLE'S IDEA OF an imaginatively designed bathroom used to be stacking towels according to colour and arranging three empty perfume bottles on the windowsill. Not any more. Bathrooms have come of decorating age, and deservedly so.

Bathrooms are a refuge from the cares of the world, where you can soak and pamper yourself with unashamed self-indulgence. To get a bathroom that you actually want to spend quality time in, you must first pamper your surroundings.

Creams, white and washed-out pastels are always popular, and for good reason — they make small areas look larger. But there's no need to adhere strictly to pale colours. What about, for example, a beach look, based upon the cool tones of a northern sea, or the saturated colours of the Mediterranean ? Brightly coloured metal beach buckets hung from a piece of driftwood should do the trick. You could cover a wall with plaster stars or create a mosaic splash-back of china. The view from the bath is looking better all the time!

What about views you don't want to see? Cover windows without losing light with fixed blinds made of translucent, woven scrim, or strips of parched wood from a broken-up orange box — simple solutions that can be created in a matter of hours.

One idea to make your bathroom a bit unusual is to use bright buckets as containers, an evocative reminder of the summer.

Re-vamp a plastic laundry basket for a fun container or for a more sophisticated look, use an antique-finished terracotta pot. To step over, rather than into, puddles of water on the floor, lay strips of raised wooden decking. It's easy, very practical, and incredibly stylish.

The ideas in this book provide a bathroom in which you can wash, shower, bathe and unwind. Whether you go for the bright beach look, the classical Roman touch or the crisp, cool serenity of Japanese style, there will be just one problem — once inside, you'll never want to leave.

SURFACES

Above: Here, visual interest is created with texture. Colours are kept to a limited monochromatic palette, while the rough-plaster effect on the wall is echoed in the decorative details.

BATHROOM SURFACES NEED TO BE practical, hygienic, easy-to-clean, and above all, waterproof. The way you treat surfaces will have a defining impact on the character of your bathroom. By decorating walls and floors, you can create almost any effect you want. To freshen a room, opt for vivid Balearic blues and greens, or to bring the wild Atlantic indoors, think of rough plaster and distressed, weather-worn silvers and whites.

Right: Plain tiles were given an aquatic motif with a simple yet effective technique. The tiles were spattered using an old toothbrush to flick the paint all over the surface. When completely dry, a stencil cut in a wave shape was laid over the top, and the spatter technique repeated to build up the colour.

Beyond paint, all kinds of techniques can be utilized to create remarkable end results. Some may appear elaborate, but the techniques required are often very simple. The ornate elegance of mosaic tiling, despite its intricate appearance, is remarkably easy to create. An even simpler option is to re-look at using tiling creatively: with the wide choice now available commercially, you can work with vivid blocks of colour or decorative patterns. If you don't find a pattern to suit your taste, you can customize plain tiles with acrylic enamel paints. However you decide to decorate your bathroom, the method in which you treat surfaces really is an easy way to make a great impression.

Above: White-washed wood is fresh and appealing in the bathroom. Use a paint with a wipe-clean finish for ease.

Left: Don't be afraid of colour. Just because the bathroom is often small doesn't mean its walls can't support intense shades. Here, tongue-and-groove panelling was painted a rich green.

SOFT FURNISHINGS

Above: Light fabrics such as butter muslin will allow natural light in a bathroom while retaining an element of privacy. Here shells with tiny holes were wired to the curtain edges.

YOU CAN ADD YOUR OWN personal style to your bathroom by embellishing it with carefully chosen and individualistic soft furnishings. Windows, doorways and even the bath itself all merit attention, and you will be richly rewarded by spending a little time on these areas.

Shower curtains can be decorated with beautiful marine motifs that will impart a hint of seashore charm. Similarly, a plain window can be dressed up to become a focal point of any bathroom. If you want softer light in the bathroom, why not use beach finds like beautiful shells and weather-beaten glass to make a striking window screen that will diffuse streaming sunlight. Unwanted beach windbreaks could find a new purpose in your home as cheerful blinds for your bathroom, or for more

Right: A clear plastic shower curtain is given a personal treatment by suspending organic items such as driftwood and starfish from natural string.

Left: Towels hanging on a drying rack provide an impromptu screen around a tin bath tub. In a larger bathroom this is a stylish way of separating different areas of the bathroom.

opulent tastes, you could use intensely coloured fabrics for a regal window treatment.

Practical concerns in the bathroom needn't restrict style. Billowing curtains can be restrained at shower time with customized tie-backs and drawstring bags are a simple yet stylish way to store laundry or towels. For somewhere to perch while waiting for that bath to run, you could turn a discarded metal bucket into a stool by adding a fabric cushion filled with lavender. The aroma will make your bathroom even more alluring, and more difficult to leave!

Below: Piles of fresh linen hand towels are a welcoming sight. Blue and white is always crisp and appealing, while sprigs of lavender pick up the colour scheme and impart a relaxing scent.

FINISHING TOUCHES

Above: Scented soaps adorned with organza ribbon bows, piled into an heirloom bowl, are a simple way to add an air of luxury.

TO MAKE YOUR BATHROOM truly a relaxing haven, pay a little attention to those finishing touches, the little additions that can make all the difference. These can be as simple as a favourite collection of glass bottles lining a windowsill or a few decorative items to complement your overall decorating scheme.

Pamper yourself and your guests with bowls of fragrant, coloured soaps, or bottles and containers of bubble baths and lotions. For a minimalist approach, fill a glass jar with pebbles or small pieces of

Right: Here, a small mosaic bowl matches a bathroom mirror. Sanddollars, dried sponge and pebbles are heaped inside.

driftwood. If you're looking for something that's fun but functional, jazz up an unsightly laundry basket with coloured beads. Anything that shows a little bit of imagination and invention will make the warmth and security of that hot bath even more enticing.

Below: Old-world charm is delightfully evoked with this porcelain jug and basin in blue and white. Stoppered bottles of scent and bath oils complete the picture.

Mosaic Splashback

MOSAICS LOOK COMPLICATED and elaborate but are actually very simple to do; you just need time and patience to complete the job. Use up broken tiles or look for chipped junk-shop finds to make a unique splashback for behind a bathroom sink. You can have as simple or as complicated a colour scheme as you wish. You need a good selection of differently sized pieces. Break up the tiles, plates and so on by putting them between two pieces of cardboard and hammering them gently, but firmly. The cardboard will prevent tiny chips from flying around. Work on a piece of backing board such as MDF or plywood so that you can sit down with the mosaic on a table, which is less back-breaking than applying the mosaic directly on to a wall.

YOU WILL NEED

tape measure

backing board, such as MDF or plywood

pencil

set square (T-square) or ruler

jigsaw

drill, with wood and masonry bits

beading (molding)

mitre block and saw or mitre saw

wood glue

white emulsion (latex) paint

household paintbrush

selection of broken tiles and ceramic fragments

glue gun and glue sticks

screws

grout

wall plugs

screwdriver

one *Measure the backing board to fit the width of your sink. Draw your chosen splashback shape on to the board using a pencil and a set square or ruler.*

two *Carefully cut out the shape using a jigsaw.*

three *Mark the position of the holes that will be used to attach the splashback to the wall. Drill the holes.*

four *Measure the beading (molding) that will frame the backing. Mitre the beading using a mitre block or mitre saw.*

five *Glue the beading in place with wood glue, following the manufacturer's instructions.*

six *When the glue is dry, paint the whole splashback white. Leave to dry.*

seven *Arrange the ceramic pieces on the splashback. Experiment until you have created a pleasing pattern.*

eight *Glue the ceramic pieces in place using the glue gun.*

nine *Put screws into the screw holes, to prevent grout getting into the holes. Grout over the mosaic, being careful near any raised, pointed bits.*

CONTINUED OVER ➤

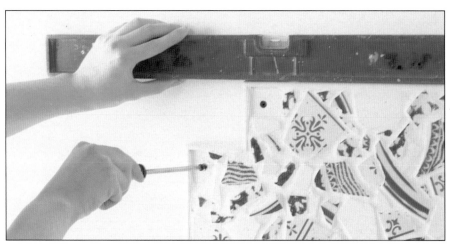

ten *Drill holes into the wall and insert the wall plugs. Then screw the splashback into position on to the wall.*

eleven *Glue on more ceramic pieces, to hide the screws.*

twelve *Re-grout over these pieces.*

BOAT SPLASHBACK

A DETACHABLE MOSAIC SPLASHBACK makes a very practical surface above a bathroom sink, being strong and durable as well as waterproof. This jaunty boat design is made entirely from broken tile mosaic – sort the pieces into groups of each colour to make it easier when you are working on the picture. Flashes of mirror tile give the splashback an extra sparkling quality.

one *Seal the front and back of the plywood with diluted PVA (white) glue. Leave to dry, then score the front of the board with a craft knife.*

two *Using a pencil, draw a simple boat design on the front of the board. Place the board on a work bench, then clamp in position. Use a bradawl to make a screw hole in each corner.*

three *Wearing protective leather gloves and goggles, wrap each tile separately in sacking and break with a hammer. Trim the pieces with mosaic nippers if necessary. Wearing rubber gloves and using a knife or flexible spreader, spread tile adhesive within the lines of the drawing. Build up the shape, leaving the portholes and windows blank.*

four *Fill in the background sea and sky with light blue tile pieces. Continue to within 1cm (¹/₂in) of the edge of the board, avoiding the screw holes.*

five *Wearing protective leather gloves and goggles, cut the white border strip into short lengths with mosaic nippers. Fill in the border around the edges of the design, working as before. Leave a gap between each border piece for grouting.*

CONTINUED OVER ➤

six *Add pieces of mirror tile to make the portholes and windows. Remove excess adhesive from the surface of the splashback with a damp sponge. Push a length of drinking straw into each hole. Leave to dry for 24 hours.*

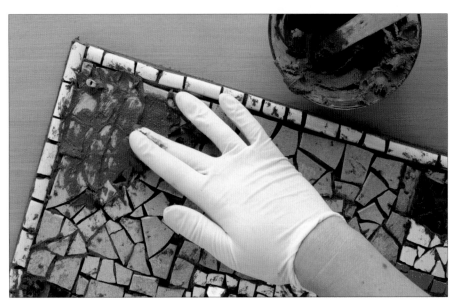

seven *Wearing rubber gloves, spread more tile adhesive over the surface, making sure any sharp edges are covered. Smooth the adhesive around the straws. Remove excess adhesive with a damp sponge, then leave the splashback to dry for 24 hours. Remove the straws. Wearing a face mask, smooth the surface lightly with a sanding block, then polish with a dry, lint-free cloth. Seal the back of the board with two coats of yacht varnish, allowing it to dry between coats.*

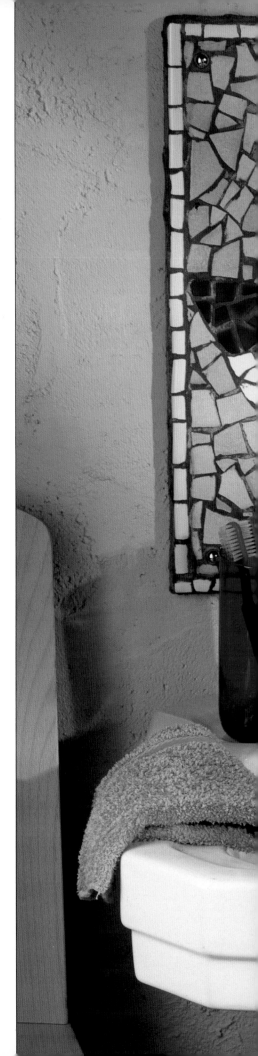

PATCHWORK-EFFECT TILES

BATHROOMS AND SHOWER ROOMS are often thought of simply as basic utility rooms because they tend to get heavily splashed and also, with today's busy lifestyle, most people spend little time there. Consequently, their floorings are frequently correspondingly spartan. However, the wide range of ceramic tiles now available enables you to achieve stunning good looks without sacrificing practicality. Here we opted for stylish blue tiles in the same colour range, accented by deep indigo.

YOU WILL NEED
pencil

ruler

tile adhesive (waterproof for bathrooms; flexible if on a suspended floor)

ceramic tiles

notched spreader

tile spacers

straight edge (optional)

squeegee

grout

damp sponge

lint-free dry cloth

dowel scrap

one *Draw a grid on the floor for the tiles. Using the spreader, spread some adhesive on an area of the floor small enough to be reached easily. Start laying the tiles. As you do so, use spacers to ensure that the gaps between them are even. Use a straight edge to check that all the tiles are horizontal and level. When all the tiles have been laid, use a squeegee to spread grout over them and fill all the join lines – this is for both appearance and waterproofing.*

two *Wipe off the surplus grout with a damp sponge before it dries.*

three *Buff with a dry cloth when the grout has hardened, then smooth the grout with the scrap piece of dowel.*

HAND-PRINTED "TILES"

THESE IMITATION TILES ARE, in fact, hand-printed on to the wall using a home-made foam stamp. This is a quicker and less expensive alternative to ceramic tiles, and there are endless colour combinations. If you opt for shades of one colour, it is inexpensive because you can buy one pot of paint and lighten it with white. Making a sponge stamp to apply the colour is a quick and foolproof way of getting squares of colour on to the wall. If you start with a white wall, the lines left between the fake tiles will look like the grouting between real tiles.

YOU WILL NEED

ruler

pencil

scrap paper

high-density foam rubber, such as upholstery foam

glue

craft knife

self-healing cutting mat

emulsion (latex) paint in 2 colours, plus white

household paintbrushes

scissors

straight edge

spirit (carpenter's) level

old plates

small roller

small brush

clear varnish

varnish brush

one *Decide on the size of the tiles. Draw your design for the stamp on paper. Glue it to the foam and cut out unwanted areas. Angle the cut outwards slightly from top to bottom. Make a stamp for each colour. For this design you need six stamps.*

two *Use smaller pieces of foam to make a handle on the back of each stamp.*

three *Choose your colours – aquatic greens and blues work particularly well in bathrooms. Here, a scheme of six shades, made from two basic colours, was used. One-third of each colour was mixed together to make a third colour, and then these three colours were halved again and lightened with white.*

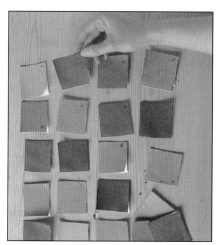

four *Decide on the repeat pattern; small-scale paper squares, painted in the different colours and shades, will help you plan the design.*

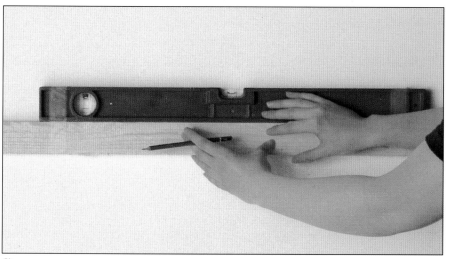

five *Mark horizontal guidelines on the wall with faint pencil lines, using a straight edge and a spirit (carpenter's) level.*

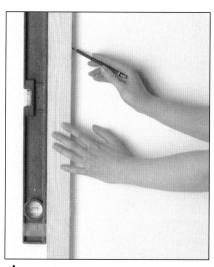

six *Mark vertical guidelines in the same way.*

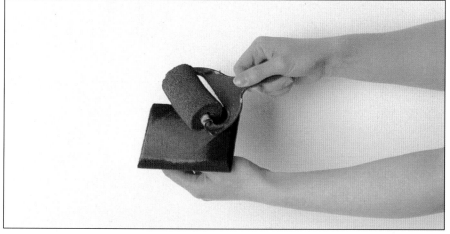

seven *Put some paint on to a plate and run the roller through it until it is evenly coated, then roll the paint on to the first stamp.*

CONTINUED OVER ➤

eight *Stamp the "tile" pattern on to the wall, pressing down firmly with your fingers. Go right around the "grout" area and touch up any stray smudges with white paint and a small brush. Make sure that no pencil guidelines are visible.*

nine *When dry, apply two coats of varnish to protect the surface and give it a wipeable finish.*

GREEK KEY BATHROOM

THIS BATHROOM LOOKS FAR TOO smart to have been decorated by an amateur. The border design is a classic Greek key interspaced with a bold square and cross. The black and gold look stunning on a pure white wall. Every bathroom has different features, so use the border to make the most of the best ones, while drawing attention away from the duller areas. If you want a co-ordinated scheme, you could print a border on a set of towels, using fabric inks.

YOU WILL NEED

tracing paper

pencil

spray adhesive

high-density foam rubber,
such as upholstery foam

scalpel

acrylic enamel paint:
black and gold

2 plates

wooden baton 2–3cm
(³/4-1¹/4in) wide, depending
on the bathroom

masking tape

one *Trace and transfer the pattern shapes from the template. Lightly spray the shapes with adhesive and place them on the foam rubber. To cut out the shapes, cut the outline first, then undercut and remove any excess, leaving the pattern shape standing proud of the foam.*

two *Apply an even coating of black paint on to a plate. Place the baton up next to the door frame to keep the border an even distance from it. Make a test print on scrap paper, then begin by stamping one black outline square in the bottom corner, at dado-rail (chair-rail) height. Print a key shape above it, being careful not to smudge the adjoining edge of the previous print.*

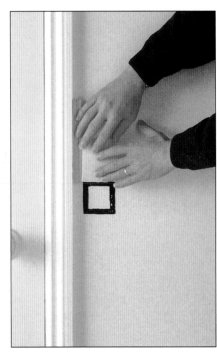

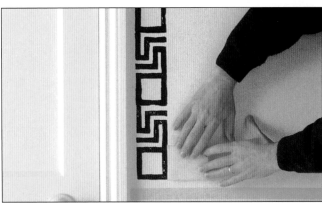

three *Continue alternating the stamps around the door. Mark the base line at the dado-rail height with masking tape and alternate the designs along this line.*

four *Place a coating of gold paint on to a plate and dip the cross shape into it. Make a test print on scrap paper, then print the shape in the square frames.*

ℬRIGHT PLASTER WALL

WALLS CAN BE GIVEN new interest and depth with this technique, which has the additional advantage of hiding any minor blemishes or unevenness. The added dimension pleasantly alters an otherwise plain surface and it is easily achieved with a little plaster filler scraped over the surface. For a much more subtle finish, the plaster filler can simply be added to the paint and brushed over the wall surface to give a very light texture. Here, a crisp white painted finish evokes whitewashed cottages by the sea, but the wall could just as well be washed over with any colour of your choosing. Experiment with turquoise and splashes of vermilion in furniture and soft furnishings, and revel in images of the sun-baked Mediterranean.

YOU WILL NEED

plaster filler

bucket

stirrer

piece of thick cardboard
or plywood

white emulsion (latex) paint

paint-mixing container
(optional)

household paintbrush

one *Following the manufacturer's instructions, mix the plaster filler in a bucket.*

two *Wipe it on to the wall with a piece of thick cardboard or plywood so that it forms an uneven surface. Leave to dry.*

three *When dry, apply a coat of emulsion (latex) paint, rubbing it in well with the paintbrush so that all the raised surfaces are thoroughly covered.*

four *Alternatively, for a slightly smoother result, mix plaster filler and emulsion paint together and brush on.*

SAILING-BOAT FRIEZE

USE THIS CHARMING YACHT bobbing on the waves to complete a bathroom with a nautical theme. It is better, if possible, to stamp tiles before fixing them to the wall, so that the ceramic paints can be made more resilient by baking in the oven. You can stamp and appliqué the same design, with embroidered details, on to your towels.

YOU WILL NEED

high-density foam rubber, such as upholstery foam

craft knife and cutting mat

ruler

stiff cardboard

PVA (white) glue and brush

pencil

graph paper

scissors

marker pen

ceramic paints in various colours

medium paintbrush

paint-mixing container

15cm (6in) square ceramic tiles

old cloth

methylated spirits (rubbing alcohol)

plain light-coloured cotton fabric

masking tape

fabric paints in various colours

embroidery hoop

stranded embroidery thread

sewing needle

iron

dressmaker's pins

hand towel

one *Cut a 15cm (6in) square and a 15 x 5cm (6 x 2in) rectangle of foam rubber to make the stamps. Cut a piece of cardboard for each square and glue one on to each piece of foam.*

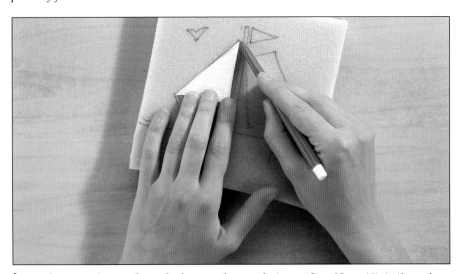

two *On scrap paper, draw the boat and wave design to fit a 15cm (6in) tile and use to make paper templates. Draw around the boat and wave designs on the square stamp using a marker pen.*

three *Cut away the excess foam around the design using a craft knife. Repeat with the wave design on the rectangular foam to make the second stamp, positioning the waves so that they will fall between the first set.*

four *Load the boat stamp with ceramic paints, applying the colours to the different areas using a paintbrush. Clean any grease from the surface of the tiles by rubbing with a cloth dipped in methylated spirits (rubbing alcohol). Allow to dry.*

five *Press the stamp over the tile. Allow to dry. Load the waves stamp and stamp another set of waves between the first set.*

six *For the wave tiles, re-load the wave stamp with paint and position it 1cm (½in) from the bottom edge. Apply the stamp, aligning it with the bottom edge. Print birds at a 45° angle above the waves.*

CONTINUED OVER ➤

seven *For the appliqué towel panel, cut out a 17cm (7in) square of fabric and tape it to the work surface. Mix fabric paints to match the ceramic paint colours and load the boat motif as before. Stamp on to the fabric and leave to dry.*

eight *Fix the paints according to the manufacturer's instructions, then insert the panel in an embroidery hoop and work a running stitch to pick out the clouds and details on the sail and boat in stranded embroidery thread.*

nine *Press under a 1cm (½in) hem all round the panel and pin it in place at one end of the towel. Work a blanket stitch all round the panel to attach it.*

ten *Stitch a pearl button to each corner of the panel, and one in the middle of each side.*

REGAL BATHROOM

DECORATING A BATHROOM ON a budget usually means that all your money goes on the bathroom suite, flooring and taps. A pure white bathroom may look clean and fresh, but a certain amount of warmth in pattern and colour is needed to prevent it from seeming too clinical. Stamping enables you to achieve a co-ordinated finish on tiles, fabric and furniture at little extra cost. If you stamp a set of tiles using acrylic enamel paint before fixing them to the wall, the design can be baked in the oven for a very hardwearing finish. If the tiles are already in place, you can use the same paint but it won't stand up to abrasive cleaning.

YOU WILL NEED

masking tape

diamond and crown stamps

pencil

emulsion (latex) paint in grey and yellow-ochre

plates

small paint rollers

wooden shelf with rail

PVA (white) glue

clear matt varnish and brush

black stamp pad

scrap paper

scissors

white cotton piqué handtowels

grey fabric paint

iron

plain white tiles

clean cloth

grey acrylic enamel paint

one *Stick a length of masking tape along the top edge of the moulding above the tiles or along the top of the tiles themselves if there is no moulding. This will give you a straight line to stamp along. Mark the position of the actual stamp in pencil, on the edge of the stamp block.*

two *Spread some grey emulsion (latex) paint on to a plate and run the roller through it until it is evenly coated. Ink the stamp and print the diamond border. Line up the pencil mark on the stamp block with the edge of the previous print so that diamonds meet without overlapping.*

three *To decorate the shelf, mix two parts yellow-ochre emulsion paint with one part PVA (white) glue. The glue will make the paint stickier and will dry to give a bright, glazed finish.*

four *Run the roller through the paint and ink the diamond stamp. The stamped design will depend on the shelf. Here, a diamond is printed on each plank to make evenly spaced rows.*

five *Stamp a crown in the centre at the top of the shelf with a diamond to either side.*

six *Seal the shelf with at least one coat of clear matt varnish.*

seven *Use the stamp pad to print 20 diamond motifs on paper and cut them out. Arrange them in three rows across the width of a towel, adjusting the spacing until you are happy with it.*

eight *Remove the top two rows of the pattern, leaving only the bottom row in place. Spread some grey fabric paint on to a plate and run the roller through it until it is evenly coated. Ink the stamp and remove each paper diamond individually as you replace it with a stamped print.*

CONTINUED OVER ➤

nine *Stamp the next row of the pattern with a diamond between each pair on the row below. Draw a central line on the back of the stamp block. Line it up with the top of the first row to help you position the second row.*

ten *Complete the border pattern with a third row of diamonds. Fix the fabric paint with a hot iron, following the manufacturer's instructions.*

eleven *Wash the tiles with detergent and dry them well. Hold the tiles by their edges to avoid fingerprints, which will repel the paint.*

twelve *Spread some grey acrylic enamel paint on to a plate and run the roller through it until it is evenly coated. Ink the crown stamp and print a single crown in the centre of each tile on the diagonal.*

ℬLISSFUL BATHROOM

SEA-GREENS AND TURQUOISE-BLUES are ideal for the watery environment of a bathroom and the floaty mood can be enhanced by the addition of coloured muslin drapes or glass jars filled with bubble bath. The walls are first colourwashed and then a cherub border is stamped in sea-green. When the border has dried, a tinted varnish is brushed on to protect it and add another watery dimension. The chair back is stamped in emulsion (latex) paint and then varnished in a different shade. The plain wooden cupboard is stamped with cherubs and rubbed back to give it an aged look.

YOU WILL NEED

emulsion (latex) paint in turquoise, cream, sea-green and pale blue

wallpaper paste

household paintbrushes

plates

small paint rollers

cherub- and swag-motif stamps

pencil (optional)

spirit (carpenter's) level (optional)

small strip of cardboard

clear water-based varnish

varnish brush

sepia artist's watercolour

wooden kitchen chair with broad back-rest

fine artist's paintbrush

wire (steel) wool

small wooden hall cupboard

clean cloth

fine-grade sandpaper

one *Paint the walls turquoise. Mix one part cream emulsion (latex) with one part wallpaper paste and four parts water. Using random brush-strokes, paint the walls. Spread some sea-green emulsion on to a plate and run a roller through it. Ink the first cherub stamp.*

two *Rest the base of the stamp block on the top edge of the picture rail or tiles, or use a pencil and spirit (carpenter's) level to mark a line as a guide. Print a row of cherubs, alternating the two stamps and using a cardboard strip to space the border. Tint the varnish with artist's watercolour and brush it over the whole wall.*

three *To stamp the chair, first paint it sea-green and leave to dry. Spread the turquoise emulsion paint on to a plate and mix in some cream paint to soften the shade. Run a roller through the paint until it is evenly coated. Ink the swag and print in the centre of the chair back. Lighten the sea-green paint further with cream and add hand-painted detail to the stamped swag with a fine paintbrush. Leave to dry. Rub back the paint with wire (steel) wool to simulate natural wear and tear. Apply a coat of varnish and leave to dry.*

four *To stamp the cupboard, first paint it in pale blue emulsion paint. Before it has dried, rub back the paint with a clean cloth so that the pale blue colour stays in the grain, but much of the wood is revealed.*

five *Rub back the paint with fine-grade sandpaper to reveal some more of the wood underneath.*

CONTINUED OVER ➤

six *Spread some sea-green emulsion paint on to a plate and run the roller through it until it is evenly coated. Ink both cherub stamps and make two prints on the door panel. Leave to dry.*

seven *Lightly rub back the cherub stamps with a cloth to give an antique look.*

CURVING ROPE DESIGN

A PATTERN IN ROPE makes a simple, textured wall finish, perfectly in keeping with today's trend for natural materials in interiors. Rope makes good curves, so the design can be as twisting as you like. For a small area in the bathroom, mark out squares and put a different, simple design in each square. You could also use the rope to create borders or frames within the bathroom at dado-rail (chair-rail) and picture-rail height.

YOU WILL NEED

scrap paper

pencil

spirit (carpenter's) level

straight edge

rope

glue gun and glue sticks or strong adhesive

masking tape

craft knife

white emulsion (latex) paint

household paintbrush

one *Plan and draw your design to scale on paper.*

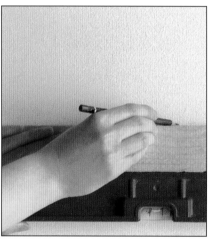

two *Transfer the design using a spirit (carpenter's) level and a straight edge.*

three *Use a glue gun or other suitable adhesive to attach the rope to the wall. Use paint cans or other round objects to help you to make smoothe curves. It is easier if you wrap masking tape around it, and cut through the tape.*

four *Paint over the wall and rope with white emulsion (latex) paint; you may need a few coats to get an even finish.*

STAR STENCIL

This misty blue colour scheme is ideal for a bathroom and the lower part of the wall is varnished to provide a practical wipe-clean surface. The tinted varnish deepens the colour and gives it a sheen that contrasts beautifully with the chalky distemper above. The stencil is based on a traditional quilting motif and is very simple to create.

YOU WILL NEED

paper and pencil
straight edge
scissors
spray mount adhesive
stencil card (cardboard)
sharp craft knife and cutting mat
soft blue distemper or chalk-based paint
household paintbrushes
spirit (carpenter's) level
straight edge
clear satin water-based varnish
varnish brush
Prussian blue artist's acrylic paint

one *Draw the star shape on paper. Spray the back lightly with adhesive, then stick it on to the stencil card (cardboard).*

two *Using a craft knife on a cutting mat, cut out the star. Cut inwards from the points towards the centre so that the points stay crisp.*

three *Peel away the paper template to reveal the stencil.*

four *Dilute the blue paint, if necessary, according to the manufacturer's instructions. Brush it on to the wall with sweeping, random strokes to give a colour-washed effect.*

five *Using a spirit (carpenter's) level, and a straight edge, draw a pencil line across the wall at the height you want to finish the varnished surface.*

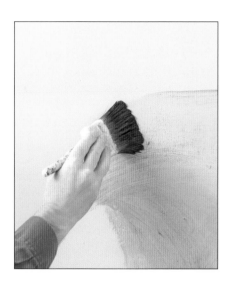

◄ **six** *Tint the varnish with a squeeze of Prussian blue acrylic paint. Using a separate brush, apply this on the lower part of the wall up to the marked line.*

seven *Spray the back of the stencil lightly with adhesive and position at one end of the wall, about 5cm (2in) above the marked line. Stencil with the tinted varnish, using a broad sweep of the brush. Repeat along the wall, spacing the stars evenly.* ➤

COLOURED WOODEN BATTENS

SOMETIMES THE SIMPLEST IDEAS are the most effective. Strips of wood spaced on the wall at regular intervals can create an unusual and very dramatic look. Use them on a single wall or in smaller areas, such as the back of an alcove. The key is to keep the colours either toning or very contrasting and bold. If time permits, paint the top and bottom of the wood in slightly different shades of the same colour to add extra interest. The strips of wood used here are 5 x 2.5cm (2 x 1in).

YOU WILL NEED

tape measure

wood strips

pencil

saw

matt emulsion (latex):
blue and white

household paintbrush

spirit (carpenter's) level

drill, with masonry and
wood bits

wall plugs

wood screws

ruler

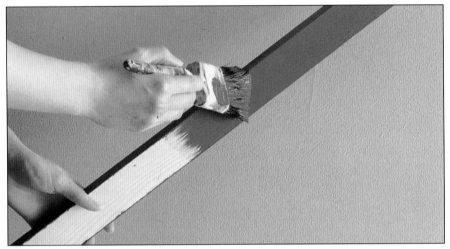

one *Measure the height and width of the wall to make sure you will have equal spacing all the way up the wall. Cut the wood strips to the required length. Paint the wood strips; you could paint all three sides that will show in different colours, for a more interesting look, or in shades of the same colour, for subtlety.*

two *Use a spirit (carpenter's) level to mark a guideline for the first strip, to make sure the wood is absolutely level.*

three *Drill holes in the wall and insert wall plugs. Drill holes in the wood and then screw the strip in place. Mark out the position for the next wood strip; the space between strips must be absolutely even to create the right effect.*

PLASTER STARS

PLASTER HAS A POWDERY quality and a pure white colour, which make it an especially interesting wall embellishment. Equally, of course, it can be painted in any colour of your choice. Most decorative plaster firms have lots of simple shapes – both modern and traditional – to choose from and will make a mould of virtually anything you like, so the possible variations of this effect are endless. This idea works well as a border above a skirting (base) board or around a door, as well as in a defined area, such as behind a wash basin, as shown here.

YOU WILL NEED
plaster stars
scissors
masking tape
clear varnish or
PVA (white) glue
household paintbrush
wall adhesive
wood scrap

one *Decide on the design and spacing of the stars (or the fancy plaster motifs of your choice) by making photocopies of them, cutting them out and using small pieces of masking tape to attach them to the wall. Try out a number of versions until you are happy with the final effect.*

two *Seal the stars with clear varnish or PVA (white) glue mixed with water.*

three *When the stars are dry, use wall adhesive to attach them to the walls. Use a wood scrap as a spacer for positioning the stars on the wall.*

FRAMED TILE PICTURES

THERE ARE SO MANY BEAUTIFUL tiles available that you may be loath to set a current favourite permanently into the wall for fear there may be a design you like more just around the corner. Here is the perfect solution: box frames containing a constantly changing display of tiles that can be hung anywhere as the fancy takes you. The backing boards can be re-painted in minutes. Foam pads are used to hold the tiles in place inside the frames. For a damp environment such as the bathroom, it is recommended to use those intended for outdoors.

YOU WILL NEED

box frames deep enough to comfortably contain a tile

diluted PVA (white) glue and glue brush

emulsion (latex) paint

medium paintbrush

set square (T-square)

ruler

pencil

exterior-strength sticky fixing pads

decorative tiles

tack hammer

panel pins (tacks)

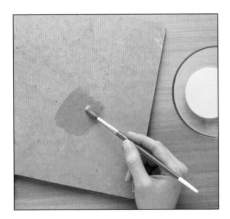

one *Seal the surface of the hardboard backing of the frame using diluted PVA (white) glue. Leave the backing to dry thoroughly.*

two *Paint the backing board with emulsion paint (latex) in the colour of your choice. You may need more than one coat to achieve a good, even surface. Leave the backing board to dry between coats.*

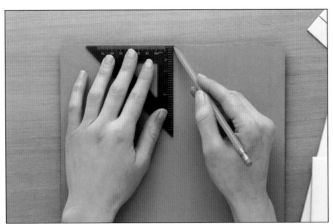

three *Using a set square (T-square) and ruler, find the centre of the backing board and mark the point with a cross.*

four *Place a sticky pad in each corner of the tile. Press the pads firmly in place and remove the backing paper.*

◄ **five** *Centre the tile over the cross in the middle of the backing board. When you are satisfied with the position of the tile, press in place.*

six *Place the frame face down. Position the board over the back of the frame and attach it, using small panel pins (tacks).* ➤

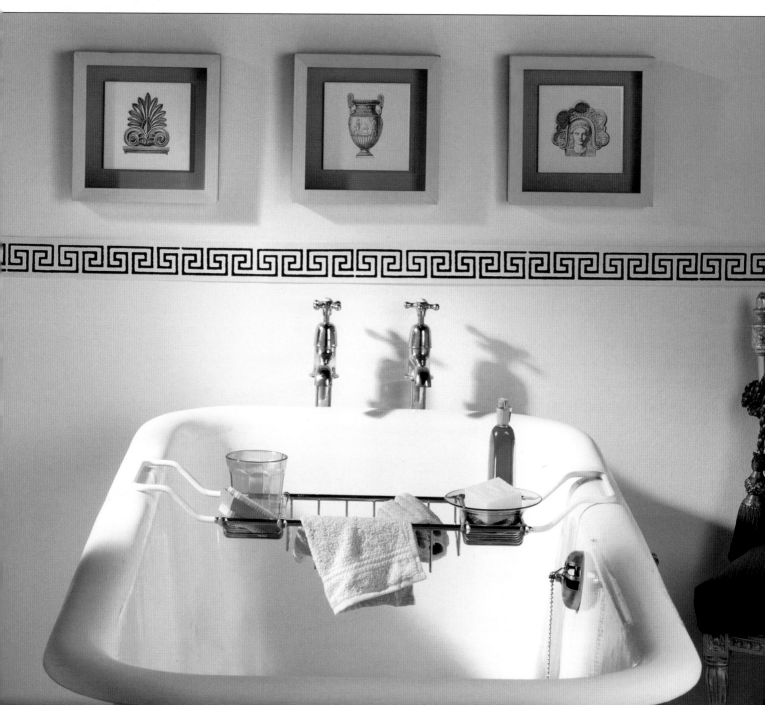

ＷOODEN DECKING

THE JAPANESE BATHHOUSE is the inspiration for this floor treatment, preventing pools of water from turning your bathroom into a skating rink and, at the same time, imparting the serenity of a Zen garden. In this project the duckboards form a pontoon or walkway across the bathroom, but you could also use sections and cut them around the bathroom fittings. Ready-made decking is also available in strips or squares.

YOU WILL NEED
tape measure
saw
quadrant beading (molding)
decking or duckboards
drill, with wood bit and pilot bit
soft cloth
household paintbrush
wood stain
wood screws

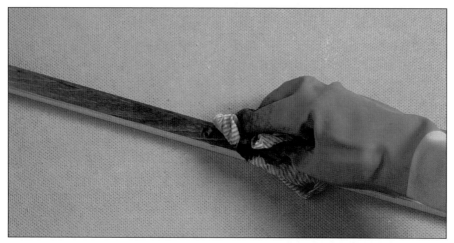

one *Make sure you have a clean, level floor: cork tiles, wood and lino are all suitable. The existing floor will show through, so if you want to change the colour, do so now! Measure and cut the two lengths of beading (molding) to the same length as the runners on the decking or duckboards. Drill holes through these new runners. Stain the two new long runners to the same colour as the decking or duckboards.*

two *Measure the distance between the runners on the decking or duckboard.*

three *Space the new runners at a distance that will allow the decking or duckboard runners to slide between them, holding the board steady but allowing it to be lifted up for cleaning. Screw in place by drilling through the subfloor, using the correct type of bit for the type of floor you have. Slide the boards into place.*

WINDOW SCREEN

THIS IS AN IDEAL SCREEN for any window which isn't overlooked, as its main purpose is decorative. It would make a lovely hanging in the watery world of the bathroom. It is an individual way of displaying seashore finds, such as worn glass, shells and stones and newer items such as fishing floats, weights and lures (with their hooks removed). Everything is fixed on with near-invisible fishing line so the screen appears to be floating in mid-air within the window space. The more you gaze at it, the more the image of the sea is brought to mind.

YOU WILL NEED

seaside finds, such as glass, shells and fishing tackle

fishing line

glue gun and sticks (optional)

bradawl

piece of dowel

hooks and rings

one *On a flat surface, lay out your selection of seaside objects in a design of your choice.*

two *Tie the objects on to lengths of fishing line, either making holes and knotting them or fixing them on with a glue gun.*

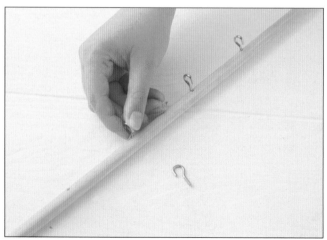

three *Using a bradawl, make holes in the dowel at regular intervals and insert hooks.*

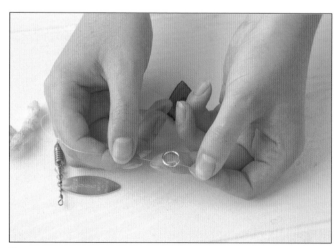

four *Attach the rings on to the ends of the decorated lines and hang them from the hooks on the dowel.*

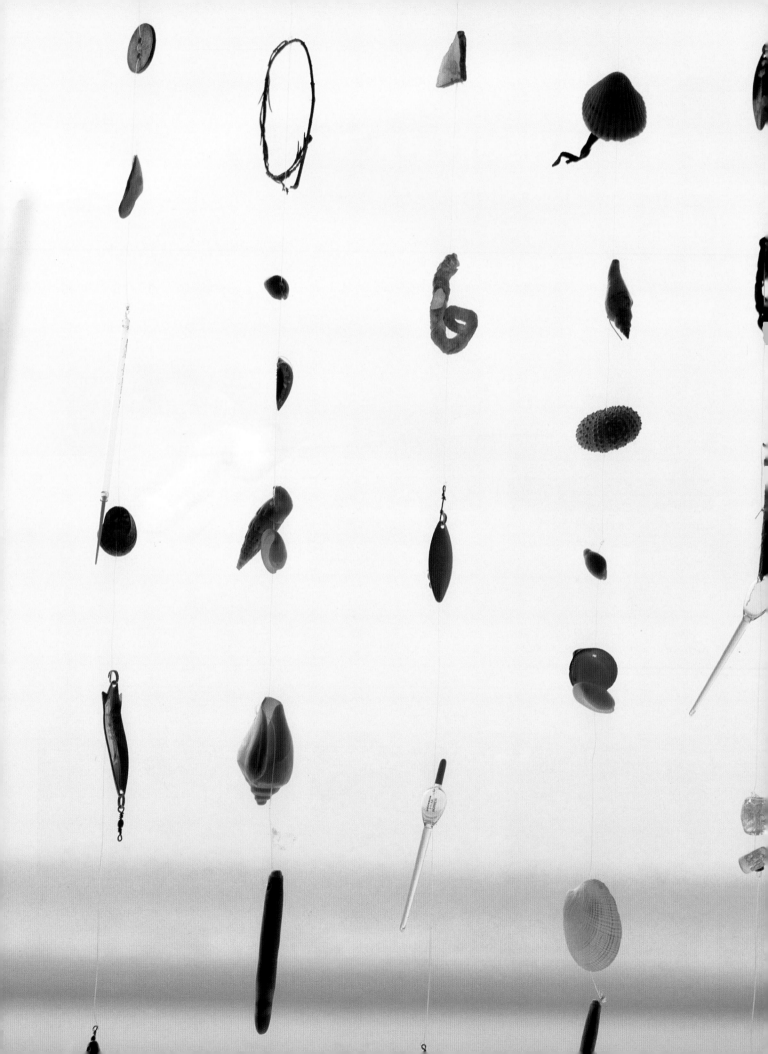

STRIKING CONTRAST

IN MOST WINDOW TREATMENTS the lining is unobtrusive, but here it becomes the focal point. The contrasting colours of these silks make an eye-catching statement, but a plain fabric with a patterned lining would look equally effective.

one *Measure the window and cut two pieces of each fabric and two pieces of interfacing to the finished size plus 2cm (³⁄₄in) seam allowance all round. Cut two 20 x 6cm (8 x 2¹⁄₂in) strips of lining fabric. Fold lengthways, right sides together, and stitch the long edge leaving a 1cm (¹⁄₂in) seam allowance. Trim the seam, turn through and press.*

two *Fold each strip in half widthways to make a loop. Pin the two raw edges of each loop to the lower inside corner of the right side of each lining piece.*

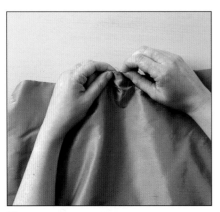

three *Place the fabric and lining right sides together, then lay the interfacing on top. Pin and stitch the edges, catching in the ends of each loop at the lower corner, and leaving a gap of 40cm (16in) in the top edge. Turn to the right side and slip-stitch the gap.*

four *At even intervals across the top edge, mark the positions of the eyelets with a fabric marker or tailor's chalk, placing one near each corner.*

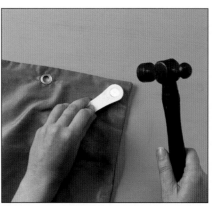

five *Using an eyelet tool and a hammer, insert the eyelets across the top edge. Cut a length of ribbon for each eyelet hole, thread it through and knot firmly to the curtain pole.*

SHELL TIE-BACKS

CURTAIN TIE-BACKS can be made in a wide range of styles so you can use them to create whatever effect you like. Though we normally think of a simple braid or tassel, tie-backs can be trimmed to make them focal points within the room – ideal in a room as small as most bathrooms. Here a fishing net was festooned with different types and sizes of shells. You could wire a mass of very small shells on to the net or even edge the curtain with a widely spaced line of matching shells.

YOU WILL NEED
fishing net

shells

fine wire

wire cutters

glue gun and glue sticks
or electric drill, with very
fine drill bit

string (optional)

one *Take the fishing net and arrange it in graceful folds. Gather together a mass of shells and see how they look best when arranged on the net. Cut lengths of fine wire. These can then be glued to the back of the shells so that they can be wired on to the netting.*

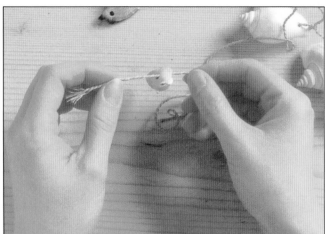

two *Alternatively, drill holes in the shells. Thread string through the holes for attaching to the net.*

three *Fix the shells on the netting. Make another tie-back in the same way. Loop the tie-backs around the curtains and on to the wall.*

VICTORIAN STENCILLING

THIS IDEA ORIGINATED from the etched glass windows of the Victorian era. You can easily achieve the frosted, etched look on plain glass by using a stencil cut from stencil card and car enamel paint. The paint needs to be sprayed very lightly, so practise on some picture frame glass first to judge the effect. The stencil design is shown here, but you could easily design your own. Look at examples of lace panels to get some inspiration.

YOU WILL NEED

tape measure

masking tape

tracing paper

stencil card (cardboard)

pencil

craft knife

brown paper

matt white car enamel spray

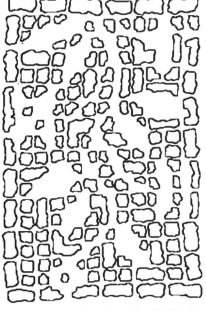

one *Measure the panes and mark the halfway points with masking tape. Photocopy and enlarge the stencil design and cut it from stencil card (cardboard). Tape the main stencil pattern in position, then use brown paper to mask off the surrounding area, at least 50cm (20in) deep on all sides. (The spray spreads further than you think.)*

two *Shake the paint can thoroughly, as this affects the fineness of the spray. Spray from a distance of at least 30cm (12in), using short puffs of spray.*

three *Depending on the dimensions of the window panes, there may be strips along the sides of the main panel that also need stencilling. This pattern has a border to fit around the edge – you may need to adapt it to fit your pane.*

ORANGE-BOX BLIND

FRUIT SHOPS ARE ACCUSTOMED to supplying raw materials to their customers, but they might be a little surprised when you ask them for their wooden boxes rather than their fresh produce! Get some orange boxes if you can, as the thin planks make ideal and original slats for blinds. These wooden blinds work best on a small, permanently obscurable window, such as in the bathroom. Although the blinds look Venetian, they don't actually pull up, but with a bit of perseverance you could probably make them do so. Here the wood was left natural, but it could be stained any colour.

YOU WILL NEED
orange boxes
pliers
sharp knife
medium- and fine-grade sandpaper
ruler
pencil
drill, and wood bit
string
scissors
2 cup hooks

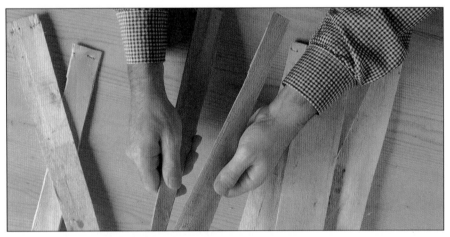

one *Pull the orange boxes apart and select the most interesting parts from the longest sides. Remove any wire staples with pliers. Split some of the planks so that the slats are not all the same size. The final effect is more successful if the pieces are intentionally irregular.*

two *Shave off some of the wood to add character to the finished blind.*

three *Use medium-grade sandpaper first and then fine-grade sandpaper to smooth the wood and round off the edges.*

four *Place the slats side by side so that the edges line up. Mark a point 5cm (2in) from each end and 3cm (1¼in) from the bottom long edge. Although the slats are different widths, the holes should be drilled through points that line up on the front of the blind.*

five *Drill through the positions you have marked. The holes should be big enough to take the string through twice, but no bigger.*

six *Begin threading the string through the blind. Go through the blind from the back and pull a long length, about twice the drop of the window. It must be threaded all the way down the blind, to include all the looping around the slats.*

seven *Loop the string back over the slat and thread it through the hole a second time.*

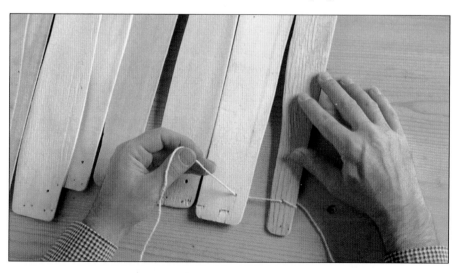

◄ eight *Take the string up through the second slat. Continue as you did with the first, looping it around and through each slat twice, working all the way down the slats.*

CONTINUED OVER ➤

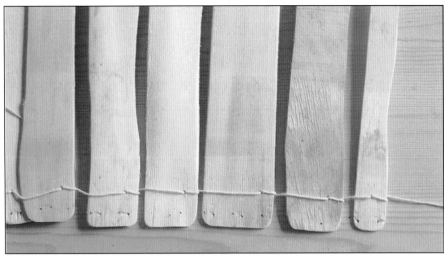

nine *When you get to the last slat, tie the string in a double knot and cut it off. Repeat this process on the other side. This is what the blind will look like from the "working side".*

ten *Turn the blind around as shown to hang it up so that you only see the string entering and leaving each slat. Screw two hooks up into the window frame and hang up the blind.*

WOVEN BLIND

THIS COLOURED MESH RIBBON is one of the new natural materials now available. It is stiff enough to hold its shape and be folded into sharp creases to make a blind. Use this treatment for a window that must be be obscured from prying eyes while still allowing maximum light to penetrate the room – a bathroom, shower room or toilet. To make the most of their interesting texture and soft colours, the ribbons have been interwoven.

YOU WILL NEED

strips of woven mesh ribbon
in 3 colours,
6cm (2½in) wide

scissors

tape measure

2 broom handles

staple gun

bradawl

2 plumbers' pipe fittings

screwdriver

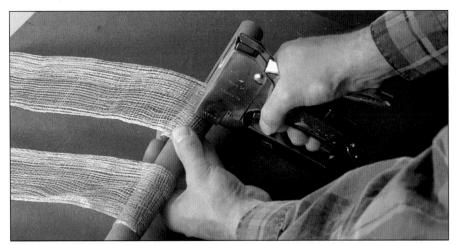

one *Cut lengths of woven mesh ribbon to the length of the drop, plus 20cm (8in). Wrap a 10cm (4in) length around a broom handle and secure it with a staple gun. Leaving 3cm (1¼in) gaps between each ribbon, continue fixing the ribbons along the broom handle with the staple gun. Finish with 9cm (3½in) of bare wood at the end. Repeat this process to fix the ends of the strips to the second broom handle.*

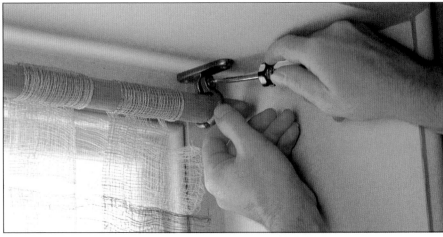

two *Cut the remaining two colours into strips to fit the width of the blind, plus a 3cm (1¼in) allowance each side. Weave these through the first ribbons.*

three *At each side, turn the seam over and crease it with your thumbnail, then staple the two ribbons together. Use a bradawl to make two small holes on either side of the underside of the top recess, then screw in the plumbers' fittings. Put the broom handle in position, then screw the front section of the fittings into position.*

HULA-HULA

ORDINARY WINDBREAKS used on the beach can be transformed into instant blinds. They come in a range of lengths with poles in pockets to divide the equal sections, just like a Roman blind, but bolder. All you have to do is saw off the extra piece of pole that goes into the sand and hang up the blind on a couple of plumbers' pipe fittings. A wide range of cheerful summer colours is available.

YOU WILL NEED

windbreak, to fit window

scissors

stapler

saw

tape measure

drill

2 wallplugs

2 plumbers' pipe fittings

screwdriver

flower garlands, elastic or rope

string (optional)

one *Hold the windbreak vertically against your window. If the drop is too long, then cut out the nylon mesh and make a new channel for the bottom pole. Fold over a hem, making sure the pole fits, and staple along the edge.*

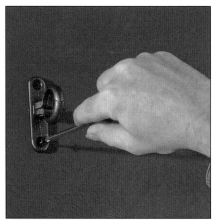

two *Saw off the excess pole, then measure the window and the top of the blind to find the position for the fixings. Drill holes and insert the wallplugs and plumbers' fittings.*

three *Hang the blind, then loop the garlands, elastic or rope between the first and last poles. If the garlands are too long, tie them in divisions with string to shorten.*

SHOWER CURTAIN

GIVE YOUR SHOWER ROOM a feel of the great outdoors with this refreshing scene of starfish, shells and seaweed swaying gently, as though rocked by an ocean current. The clear shower curtain provides a watery backdrop for you to create your very own seaside mood with whatever marine motifs you choose. The example shown here uses a monochromatic, crisp scheme, but you could equally well work with warm, bright, vivid colours to create a lively Mediterranean feel.

YOU WILL NEED
pencil
paper
scissors
masking tape
clear plastic shower curtain
white waterproof paint
artist's paintbrush

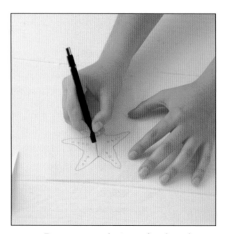

one *Draw your designs freehand on to paper, or trace a selection of seaside motifs.*

two *Reduce or enlarge the images to fit your chosen design for the shower curtain.*

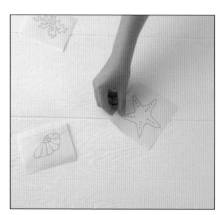

three *Cut out the paper templates or designs and arrange them on a large table top as desired. Use a table with a tough surface that won't be harmed by masking tape.*

four *Secure the paper templates in the desired position on the table top with masking tape.*

five *Place the shower curtain over the top of the images and tape it down firmly. Using white waterproof paint, carefully paint the images on to the shower curtain surface. Leave to dry thoroughly before hanging up.*

PACKING-CRATE SHELVES

THESE CHARMINGLY RUSTIC SHELVES are created from a cast-off pallet. Pallets can be picked up easily and very cheaply from timber merchants. The charm of these shelves is that they have a rather naive quality, so there's no need to be worried if the edges are a bit uneven and rough – that's all part of the effect. To finish the shelves off, wash them with a diluted emulsion (latex) paint in the colour scheme of your choice: try strong Mediterranean colours or a soft grey-blue for a touch of New England. The end result is ideal for storing toiletries or displaying seashore finds such as shells and pebbles.

YOU WILL NEED

pallet or orange box

ruler

pencil

saw

wood glue

hammer

nail

sandpaper

length of square-edged dowel

drill (optional)

string (optional)

one *Decide on what size you want your shelves to be. Measure and cut the shelf and back to the same size from the pallet or orange box. Saw two small pieces for the side sections.*

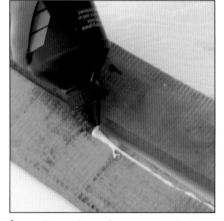

two *Run a line of strong wood glue down the back edge of the base of the shelf. Press the two pieces of wood firmly together to create a right angle. Leave to dry thoroughly.*

three *Insert the end-pieces into the right angles at either end of the shelf and hammer three nails in each side to fix firmly in place.*

four *Sand the wood down to give a smooth surface for the paint.*

five *Take the length of dowel and fix it in position with nails to form a rail across the front of the shelf.*

six *For another style of shelf, drill a hole through each end-piece and thread a piece of string through, knotting the string at each end to secure.*

STARFISH CHAIR

OLD WOODEN CHAIRS ARE NOT expensive and, with a bit of careful hunting round second-hand shops, you should be able to find yourself a real bargain. Take the time to strip the old layers of paint – it might take some time, but it gives you a much better base to work on. This chair was painted white, then it was dragged with yellow-ochre in the direction of the grain before being stamped in light grey. Choose colours that complement your bathroom scheme so that your chair will blend in.

YOU WILL NEED

medium-grade sandpaper

wooden chair

emulsion (latex) paint:
white, yellow-ochre and
light grey

paintbrush

old plate

small roller

starfish-motif stamp

clear matt varnish

varnish brush

one *Sand the chair, then apply a coat of white emulsion (latex). Mix a thin wash of five parts water to one part yellow-ochre emulsion. Use a dry brush to drag a little glaze at a time in the direction of the grain. Keep drying the brush as you work, to ensure you do not apply too much glaze.*

two *Spread some light grey paint on to the plate and run the roller through it until it is evenly coated. Ink the starfish stamp and print around the edge of the chair seat so that the design overlaps on to the sides.*

three *Fill in the seat area with starfish stamps, rotating the stamp to a different angle after each print. Space the stamps quite close together to make a dense pattern. Leave to dry thoroughly before applying a coat of varnish to protect the surface.*

FISH FOOTSTOOL

THIS LOW STOOL decorated with the leaping fish motif looks good in a bathroom but can be used anywhere in the house where you need to put your feet up. Any small and useful stool that looks as if it is handmade can be a suitable candidate for this treatment. The fish and border blocks are cut from high-density sponge, and the primitive designs, printed in off-white and light and dark blue, make patterns reminiscent of Balinese batik prints.

YOU WILL NEED

small stool

emulsion (latex) paint: dark blue, light blue and off-white

household paintbrushes

tracing paper and pencil

scalpel

spray adhesive

high-density foam rubber

scrap paper and plate

one *Give the stool two coats of dark blue paint and leave to dry. Draw the pattern shapes for the fish and border designs and cut out. Spray the shapes with adhesive and glue to the foam. Cut around the outlines and scoop out the details.*

two *Print five fish shapes on to paper and cut them out. Use them to plan the position of the fish on the stool.*

three *Apply off-white paint to the top half of the fish and light blue to the bottom.*

four *Make a test print then stamp the fish lightly on the stool, printing both colours at the same time.*

five *Paint the border stamp using the off-white paint. Stamp the design in a slightly haphazard fashion.*

BUCKET STOOL

FLORIST'S BUCKETS in galvanized tin are widely available in a variety of heights; obviously, the taller they are, the better. Cover the metal seat pad in any fabric (a waffle towel was used here). For a bathroom you could fill clear plastic fabric with fun sponges in novelty shapes. Tea (dish) towels also make fun covers and a layer of dried lavender would make a lovely scented seat.

YOU WILL NEED

1m (1yd) heavy cord or rope

2 florist's buckets

glue gun

very large self-cover buttons

scraps of material for covering buttons

fabric-cutting tool for buttons

waffle hand towel

circular cushion pad

large needle

matching sewing thread

one *Attach the cord or rope to the top rim of one of the buckets with the glue gun.*

two *Place this bucket inside the second bucket, applying glue to its rim, then invert both buckets.*

three *Use the fabric and fabric-cutting tool to cover the buttons as per the manufacturer's instructions.*

four *Sew the buttons to the centre of the waffle hand towel. Then use the towel to cover the cushion pad. Instead of smoothing out the gathering in the fabric, accentuate it, using the buttons as a focus. Glue the pad to the upturned bucket.*

MOSES BASKET

THESE GENEROUS-SIZED WOVEN BASKETS were originally designed as easy, convenient and comfortable transport for young babies. Sadly, these old-fashioned cradles do not conform to stringent modern safety regulations, so present-day newborns have safer, but rather less charming, plastic and metal contraptions instead. Moses baskets are not completely redundant, however. They are used here as fresh and airy hanging containers for clothes and also provide an attractive decorative feature for a bathroom. Alternatively you could use them for easy toy storage in a child's nursery.

YOU WILL NEED

plank of wood

tape measure

saw

sandpaper

drill, with wood and masonry bits

1 long or 2 short branches (or poles)

penknife (or wood carving knife)

dowel (optional)

2 Moses baskets

wood glue

hammer

wallplugs and screws

screwdriver

one *Cut two squares of wood at least 12 x 12cm (4¾ x 4¾in) and 5cm (2in) deep. Sandpaper the edges and drill a hole through the middle of each square, slightly smaller than the diameter of the branches. Carve away the branch ends so that they fit tightly into the holes. Sandpaper them slightly.*

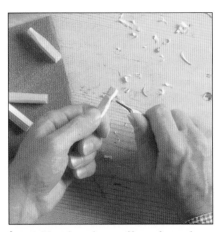

two *Use dowels or offcuts from the branches for the pegs. Taper the ends.*

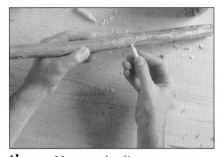

three *Measure the distance across the basket, between the basket handles, and drill two holes the same distance apart on top of each branch. Apply wood glue to each branch and tap them into each square.*

four *Apply wood glue to the peg ends and fit them into each branch. To fix the top branch to the wall, drill holes in the four corners of the square of wood, and four corresponding holes in the wall. Using the wallplugs and screws, screw the branch to the wall. Fix the lower branch to the wall allowing about 10cm (4in) clearance between the two baskets.*

ℬEADED LAUNDRY BASKET

BRIGHTLY COLOURED PLASTIC laundry baskets are cheap and practical, but they need help to give them a more individual look. This purple laundry basket was made glamorous with bright Chinese checker pieces taken from an inexpensive children's set. They are ideal as the domed pieces have spiked backs that can be trimmed to the required depth and glued into holes drilled in the plastic. The fixing is very secure, so don't worry about beads scattering all over the bathroom floor! This decorated basket is not suitable for children under three, who might swallow the checker pieces.

YOU WILL NEED
Chinese checker pieces
wire cutters
plastic laundry basket with lid
drill, with fine bit
glue gun and glue sticks
(or all-purpose glue)
masking tape

one *Sort the Chinese checker pieces into colours. Trim the spikes so that the pieces will fit into the depth of the plastic basket without protruding on the other side.*

two *Drill holes for the spikes – a circle on the lid and lines down the sides.*

three *Sort the pieces into the colour sequence you want. Apply glue to one spike at a time and push it into a hole. The glue sets quickly, so work fast.*

four *Run a length of masking tape round the base of the basket as a positioning guide for a straight band of coloured pieces. Fix these as you did the other pieces.*

TERRACOTTA LAUNDRY POT

LAUNDRY IN A FLOWERPOT? It certainly sounds unusual, but this idea makes a refreshing change from the ubiquitous wicker basket in the bathroom. Terracotta pots are now available in a huge range of shapes and sizes and a visit to your local garden centre should provide you with just the right pot. To give a pristine pot an antique feel, follow these simple steps. This project would look good in a bathroom with a Mediterranean decor.

YOU WILL NEED
large terracotta flowerpot
rag
shellac button polish
white emulsion (latex) paint
household paintbrushes
scouring pad
sandpaper (optional)

one *Soak a rag in button polish and rub all over the surface of the pot with it. The polish will sink in very fast, leaving a yellow sheen.*

two *Mix white emulsion (latex) paint with an equal quantity of water. Stir it thoroughly and apply a coat to the pot. Allow the paint wash to dry.*

three *Rub the pot with the scouring pad to remove most of the white paint. The paint will cling to the crevices and along the mouldings to look like limescale. Either leave the pot like this or rub it back further with sandpaper to reveal the clay. When you are happy with the effect, apply a coat of button polish to seal the surface.*

BATHROOM BUCKETS

ADD AN ELEMENT OF seaside fun to your bathroom – as well as useful extra storage for all those odd-shaped items – by hanging up this row of bright buckets. This trio of enamel-painted buckets was bought from a toy shop, but you could take a trip to the seaside where you are bound to find a great selection of buckets in all shapes and sizes. While there, go for a stroll along the shore to find the ideal pieces of driftwood to fix to your wall.

YOU WILL NEED

3 enamel-painted buckets
(or plastic seaside ones)

length of driftwood
(or an old plank)

pencil

drill, with wood and masonry bits

wire

pliers

wire cutters

masking tape

wall plugs and screws

screwdriver

one *Line the buckets up at equal distances along the wood. Make two marks, one at each end of the handle where it dips, for the three buckets. Using the wood bit, drill through the six marked positions to make holes through the wood.*

two *Wind wire round each handle end and poke it through the holes. Twist the two ends together at the back to secure. Trim the ends. Then drill a hole near each end of the wood.*

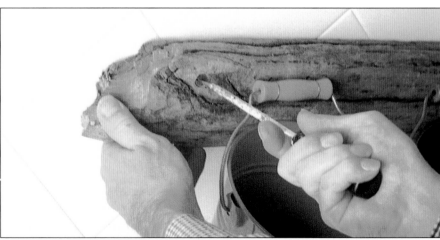

three *Hold the piece of wood in place and mark the positions for the fixings. Place a small piece of masking tape over the tile to prevent it from cracking, then drill the holes and fix the wood to the wall.*

SEA-SHELL BOX

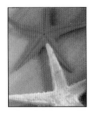

BOXES DECORATED WITH sea shells can be used for completing a sea-themed bathroom and are ideal for storing essential toiletries that you may not wish to have on view. Shells are naturally beautiful and there are endless ways of arranging them tastefully. This project combines the contemporary look of corrugated cardboard with a dynamic shell arrangement. For the finishing touch, the box is painted pure white matt.

YOU WILL NEED

selection of sea shells

round corrugated cardboard box with lid

glue gun with glue sticks (or all-purpose glue)

white acrylic paint or gesso primer

household paintbrush

one *Lay out all the shells and sort them into different shapes and sizes. Arrange them on the lid to make the design. Remove the top layer of shells from the middle of the lid and begin sticking them on. Heat the glue gun and glue the outside shells first, gradually moving inwards.*

two *Work with the shell shapes, building up the middle section. The glue gun allows you to get an instant bond, so the shells will stick to the surface however you want them to.*

three *Paint the box and the lid white. If you are using acrylic gesso primer, two coats will give a good matt covering. If you are using ordinary acrylic, the box will benefit from an extra coat of paint.*

PRETTY POTS

MINIATURE TOPIARY WILL LOOK both eye-catching and charming on a windowsill or collected together on a bathroom shelf, but don't forget to make the most of their containers. Terracotta pots have their own special appeal, but can also be treated to a variety of embellishments, from tassels to tape. Subtle, natural colours are best as they co-ordinate with the pots themselves.

YOU WILL NEED
florist's dry foam block
sharp knife
3 old terracotta pots
2 straight twigs
glue gun and glue sticks
2 florist's dry foam balls
fresh foliage, such as box
or privet
selection of pebbles
curtain weight
fine string
string tassels
masking tape
craft knife
self-healing cutting mat
matt varnish
varnish brush

one *Cut the florist's foam blocks in half and cut each block to fit into the pots. Position the foam in the pots. Insert the twigs and then glue them in place, to act as the stems of the trees. Glue the foam balls on top.*

two *Cut small pieces of foliage to the required size and insert them at random in the foam balls, to create a casual, carefree effect.*

three *Cover the foam in the pots with a layer of small pebbles so that it is completely concealed.*

four *Thread the curtain weight on to string and tie it around one of the pots. Decorate the other pots with tassels or designs cut from masking tape with a craft knife. Varnish to make the masking tape secure.*

ALL THE TRIMMINGS

DRAWSTRING BAGS ARE PERFECT for storing linen, laundry or towels, and are available from many houseware departments. Personalize your own with cheerful primary colours of blue and red, for a crisp, clean look with a slightly nautical feel. Equally, you can trim black with white for classic appeal. Felt is an easy and inexpensive way to trim plain fabrics – you could continue the scheme on bathroom curtains.

YOU WILL NEED
round template
2 squares of red felt,
about 20 x 20cm (8 x 8in)
2 squares of blue felt,
about 20 x 20cm (8 x 8in)
dressmaker's pins
fabric marker
pinking shears
blue cord
string
needle
matching sewing thread
drawstring bag

one *Find a round template: it could be a tin lid, coin or anything similar. Place the template on the felt, and draw round the template with a fabric marker. Cut around the circle with pinking shears.*

two *Pin two circles together, knot short lengths of cord and sew them on to the circles.*

three *Repeat with lengths of string. Sew the circles on to the linen bag.*

INDEX

ACKNOWLEDGEMENTS
The publishers would like
to thank the following for
creating additional projects
in this book:

Helen Baird: pp 18–21
Petra Boase: pp 32–3
Marion Elliot: pp 52–3
Judy Smith: pp 24–5,
    48–9, 50–1
Andrea Spencer: pp 30–1,
    54–5, 56–7, 62–3, 72–3,
    74–5, 92–3, 94–5

Additional photography by:
Michelle Garrett: pp 12 top
    right, 13 bottom left
Tim Imrie: p 11 bottom left
Lizzie Orme: pp 32–3
Spike Powell: pp 8 top left,
    9, 10, 12 bottom right, 13
    top right, 30–1, 72–3,
    74–5
Adrian Taylor: pp 8 bl,
    18–21; 52–3
Polly Wreford: p 11 top
    right